The
NATURE
of a
GOD-SENT
REVIVAL

By
Duncan Campbell

Copyright©: Printed by Permission
ISBN: 0-942889-05-3

PREFACE

In our day of spiritual superficiality and anemic Christianity, characterized by sin-infested pulpits and indifferent pews, the subject of revival is nonetheless a popular one. Few who talk of it, however, have the faintest idea what a real moving of God is all about. Impressive financial holdings, ornate edifices of worship, statistical proofs of "success," and mind-boggling technological sophistications merely mask the spiritual bankruptcy within the Church as a whole today. We are indeed poor in spirit. The real problem is, we seem completely incapable of even beginning to recognize just how spiritually poor we have become. We lean to our own understanding, make peace with our pet sins, deem ourselves to be rich and increased with goods and in need of nothing, all the while piddling piously with ideas of revival.

But revival can never be piddled with. It is very, very costly. Duncan Campbell, in this heart-stirring message of personal and corporate revival, strikes the taproot of the genuine working of God among His people. Such revival is rare, priceless, and exceedingly costly. Campbell captures the spirit of God's desire to work, and carefully delineates both God's sovereign moving and man's responsibility to respond to the promptings of the Spirit of God.

This world has witnessed God's sovereign dealings through the humblest of men, often at the darkest hours in history. We remember the rebirth of Martin Luther and the Reformation that followed. The Puritans obeyed God's Word with abandonment in the midst of a wicked generation. The Spirit moved mightily upon the congregation of the dry preacher Jonathan Edwards and affected an entire generation. The eighteenth century saw the powerfully convicting work of God's Spirit in New England, the nineteenth had its great New York prayer revival and the early twentieth century heralded a phenomenal spiritual awakening in Wales.

The cry of our day is, "Where is the Lord God of Elijah?" The question might better be asked, "Where are the Elijahs of the Lord God?"

While there is much prayer today, there is little of the humility behind it that characterized the life of Duncan Campbell. Here is a message by this great servant of our century. It is hot with the breath of God. It needs to be read and reread upon our knees until it burns its way into the hearts of the people of God and out through our lives. The truth is here to kindle the flame. Are we ignitable? May God once again drench us with the oil of the Spirit and set us ablaze!

The NATURE of a
GOD-SENT REVIVAL
(A MESSAGE BY DUNCAN CAMPBELL)

INTRODUCTION

Now will you turn with me to a very familiar passage of scripture. You will find it in the book of Psalms. And together we shall read Psalms 85:

Lord, thou has been favorable unto thy land; thou hast brought back the captivity of Jacob. Thou hast forgiven the iniquity of thy people, thou hast taken away all thy wrath; thou hast turned Thyself from the fierceness of thine anger. Turn us, O God of our salvation, and cause thine anger toward us to cease. Wilt thou be angry with us forever? Wilt thou draw out thine anger to all generations? Wilt thou not revive us again; that thy people may rejoice in thee? Shew us thy mercy, O Lord, and grant us thy salvation. I will hear what God the Lord will speak; for he will speak peace unto his people, and to his saints; but let them not turn again to folly. Surely his salvation is nigh them that fear him; that glory may dwell in our land. Mercy and truth are met together; righteousness and peace have kissed each other. Truth shall spring out of the earth; and His righteousness shall look down from heaven. Yea, the Lord shall give that which is good; and our land shall yield her increase. Righteousness shall go before him; and shall set us in the way of his steps.

The Lord will bless that reading from His Word.

Now, will you turn with me to verse 6. We might read verses 5 and 6. "Wilt thou be angry with us forever? Wilt thou draw out thine anger to all generations? Wilt thou not revive us again that thy people may rejoice in thee?"

I mentioned the other evening that I would be speaking this afternoon on principles that govern spiritual quickening, and I would also tell you something of how God in mercy met with me and brought revival to this heart and life of mine.

"Wilt thou not revive us again that thy people...thy people...may rejoice in Thee." These words of the Psalmist express the heart cry of many of God's dear children today. There is without question a growing conviction in many quarters that unless revival comes, that is, a God-sent revival, other forces that are out to defy every known Christian principle will take the field.

Indeed, the observant eye can already see shadows around the world that are ripening and ripening fast for repentance or judgment. With that conviction there seems to be a growing hunger for God to manifest His power, and so intense is the hunger and manifest His power, and so intense is the hunger and so deep the longing that the cry of the prophet of old is frequently heard upon the lips of God's children.

OUR ONLY HOPE IS REVIVAL

"Oh, that thou wouldest rend the heavens, that thou wouldest come down that the mountains might flow down at thy presence" (Isa. 64:1,2). You will observe that in that prayer of the prophet two fundamental things are suggested. That unless God comes down, mountains will not flow and sinners will not tremble. But if God comes down, if God manifests His power, if God shows His hand, if God takes the field, mountains will flow...mountains of indifference, mountains of materialism, mountains of humanism, will flow before His presence, and nations, not just individuals, but nations, shall be made to tremble.

We haven't seen nations trembling, but we have seen communities; we have seen districts; we have seen parishes in the grips of God in a matter of hours when God comes down!

It is true that we have seen man's best endeavor in the field of evangelism leaving communities untouched. We have seen crowded churches. We have seen many professions. We have seen hundreds, yes, and thousands responding to what you speak of here as the altar call. But I want to say this, dear people, and I say it without fear of contradiction, that you can have all that without God! Now, that may startle you, but I say again, you can have all that on mere human levels!

Howard Spring was right when he wrote, "The kingdom of God is not going to advance by our churches becoming filled with men, but by men in our churches becoming filled with God." And there's a difference! Oh, no! Crowded churches, deep interest in church activity is possible on mere human levels leaving the community untouched!

The Difference Between Evangelism and Revival

The difference in successful evangelism, (and I use the word 'successful,') and revival is this: In evangelism, the two, the three, the ten, the twenty, and possibly the hundred make confessions of Jesus Christ, and at the end of the year you are thankful if half of them are standing. But the community remains untouched. The public houses are crowded, the dances, dancing ballrooms, packed. The theater and the picture houses are patronized by the hundreds. No change in the community!

But in revival, when God the Holy Ghost comes, when the winds of heaven blow, suddenly the community becomes God-conscious! A God-realization takes hold of young, middle-aged and old. So that, as in the case of the Hebrides Revival, 75% of those saved one night were saved before they came near a meeting!

"The fear of God is the beginning of wisdom."

That is where the difference comes in between evangelism and revival, and that is why I say our only hope is not in crusades. Thank God for all that has been accomplished! Thank God for all that is being done through missions! I represent a mission in Scotland. We have also workers in Canada, and we thank God for all that is being accomplished through the efforts of ministers and evangelists and Christian workers, bringing one here and two there to a saving knowledge of Jesus. But our supreme need and the only answer to the problem that confronts the Christian church today is a visitation from God!

Revival at Berneray

Let me illustrate what I mean by an incident that happened, not in Lewis, or Uist, but on the small island of Berneray. I was addressing the Bangor Convention. The Bangor Convention is perhaps one of the largest conventions in Britain. I was sitting in the pulpit beside the chairman of the convention and the other speaker when I was suddenly gripped by the conviction that I had to leave the convention, and leave at once, and go to this island. I turned to the chairman and told him my convictions. "Oh," he said, "you cannot leave the convention. You are down to give the closing address." Oh, but I couldn't give the closing address with this conviction! So, to make a long story short, it was agreed that I should leave the convention. I left the following morning by plane to the city of Glasgow, and from Glasgow by plane to the town of Stornoway, and then by car across the island where a ferry boat met me and took me to this island of, say, 500 inhabitants.

On arriving, I met a young lad. I said nothing to the man who ferried me across. They were strangers to me. I was never on the island. I was never invited to the island, and to my knowledge no one on the island had ever met me. But I was there. And I said to the man that met me, "Would you direct me to the nearest minister?"

"We have no minister on the island. Just now both churches are vacant."

"Would you then direct me to the nearest elder?"

"Yes, the nearest elder lives in that house on the hill."

So I said to the lad, "Do you mind going up to the elder and telling him that Mr. Campbell has come to the island? And if he asks, 'What Campbell?' tell him the Campbell that was on the Island of Lewis."

So that young lad went up and after a few minutes came back and said, "Hector McKennon was expecting you to arrive today. And you are to stay with his brother. And he asked me to tell you that he has initiated a meeting at the church at 9:00 tonight and he expects you to address it."

The Secret of Revival at Berneray
Now, explain that as you will. Here was a man who on the morning of the day that I sat in the church of Bangor Island, decided to spend the day in prayer.

He was concerned about the parish, particularly about the state of the young people growing up in a state of indifference to God and to the church. And his wife told me that on three occasions she went to the door of the barn where he was praying and she heard him pray, "God, I do not know where he is, but you know, and you send him."

About 10:00 that evening he was possessed of the conviction that God heard his cry and that I would be on the island on this particular day. Hence, the initiation that I would preach in the church at 9:00 that evening.

We went to the church. Quite a considerable congregation gathered—about 80. The service was a very ordinary service. Indeed, at the end, I wondered after all if I was led to the island. But there were men there nearer to God than I was. My dear people, we've got to be honest!

This old man that I already referred to came to me and said, "I hope you are not disappointed that revival has not come to the church tonight. But God is hovering over us, and He will break through any minute!"

Here was a man near to God! *"The secret of the Lord is with them that fear Him."*

God Has Come!

We are now walking down from the church. The church is on a hillock, the main road is down about 300 yards below the church. The congregation is moving down and we are walking behind them when suddenly...oh, this is what I am getting at, *noting the difference between evangelism and revival* ...suddenly, the elder stands, takes off his hat, "Stand, Mr. Campbell. God has come! God has come! See what is happening!" And I looked toward the congregation and I saw them falling on their knees among the heather. I heard the cries of the penitent. And that meeting that began at 11:00 that night continued on the hillside until 4:00 in the morning.

The island was suddenly gripped by God! Was it because Campbell went to the island? Banish the thought!

I thank God for the privilege, and how thankful I am that I was near enough to God in that pulpit to hear His voice. I have often thought of that. Oh, I've often thought of it! If I was out of touch with God—if I was in the place where I couldn't hear the voice of the Saviour, the voice of God, would Berneray have missed that mighty visitation that shook that island from center to circumference?

I question if there was one single house on the island that wasn't visited that night! An awareness of God, a consciousness of God, seemed to hover over the very atmosphere! The very atmosphere seemed to be charged with the power of Almighty God! That is Revival!

Note the principle brought into operation. *"If my people called by my name, humble themselves, and pray, and seek my face, and turn from their wicked ways, then will I in heaven hear, come, and heal their land."*

There was at least *one* man on that island who fulfilled the conditions of that one passage of Scripture, and because he fulfilled the conditions, God, being a covenant-keeping God, must be true to His covenant engagements. And God, to vindicate His own honor, had to listen to the prayers of the parish postman who knelt in a barn for a day.

The principles that govern spiritual quickening...Oh, that God may find a people ready to fulfill and to comply with the governing principles relative to spiritual quickening.

THE ORIGIN OF REVIVAL

Now, let me touch first of all on the origin of revival. You have it in this verse. *"Wilt **Thou** not revive us again."*

My dear people, we do well to remember that in the whole field of Christian experience, *the first step is, and remains, with God.* We want to remember that. Thought, feeling, endeavor must find their basis, must find their inspiration in the sovereign mercy of God. Now I believe that. I believe it with all my heart.

I remember making that statement at a conference outside London some time ago. And at the close of the conference the chairman overheard a certain titled lady say, "That was a wonderful address that we listened to, but I don't agree with all that he said, particularly to the sovereignty of God. But we must not forget that the dear man was born and brought up among the hills of Scotland, and that is his background and he can't help it."

My dear people, let me say again, in the field of revival, God is sovereign! But, I hasten to say, that *I do not believe in any conception of sovereignty that nullifies man's responsibility.* God is the God of revival, but we are the human agents through which revival is possible. And God found that man in the postman of Berneray.

I believe this to be the reason for so few making contact with Christ that is vital: to me, one of the most disturbing factors of present-day evangelism, (let me say, present-day evangelism) is the overemphasis on what man can do. "Come to the front. Raise your hand. Respond to the altar call. Come to Jesus and be happy!" God have mercy on us! I say, God have mercy on us! Man, in the final analysis, can do nothing but throw himself on the sovereign mercy of God! Oh, let's get that clear. That is not Highland Theology. It's New Testament Theology! It's Old Testament Theology! I'm tired, positively tired of this gospel of simple believism!

The Difference Between Human Faith and Saving Faith

Oh, there is a difference between human faith and saving faith!

I heard a prominent evangelist in Britain say

something that really startled me. He said, "You exercise faith in a plane. You go into that plane and you exercise faith that that plane will take you to your destination. You go into a steamer and you exercise faith in the steamer and the captain and the crew to take you to your destination. Exercise that faith in the promises of God." Did you ever hear or listen to such nonsense? That is human faith! It is not given by God!

Oh, Calvin was right, and I love to quote him, although I am not an extreme Calvinist—though I'm a Highlander. Calvin said, "We are saved through faith alone, but the faith that saves is never alone." God is in it! Surely that is what Paul tells us in that great passage. *"I am crucified with Christ, nevertheless I live. Yet not I, but Christ, He liveth in me. And the life that I now live in the flesh I live by the"*— faith of Paul? Oh, no! That wouldn't get him very far. *"I live by the faith of the Son of God!"* The faith of God.

Harvests of Infidels or Believers?

Now I'm convinced of this, that if this truth was stressed, there would be less appeals. If this truth was stressed, our crusades and campaigns would not be producing *harvests of infidels.*

If men and women would but recognize that glorious truth—*"They shall seek me and shall find me when they shall search for me with all their heart."* That means that they may not find Him tonight. They may not find Him tomorrow night. They may not find Him next week. They may not find Him for a month or for six months, but if they are seeking God with all their hearts, they're going to find Him, or God is not true to His covenant engagement.

Oh, let's get this clear. It comes into revival. That is why I could count upon my five fingers all that I spoke to about their souls during the whole of the three years I was in the midst of it (1949-53).

You see, in the Northwest of Scotland, if you were to press yourself and your advice and your help upon an anxious soul, he would be inclined to believe that it was man's work...just man's work. And he would much rather be left to God so that God Himself would handle him. That is why we have known people for weeks and longer in distress of soul before light broke in upon them.

No Backsliders

You go back to those villages today—I'm glad I see Mr. McFarland of the Faith Mission here. He was up on Lewis not so very long ago. He was in a village that saw the mighty movings of God. I never spoke to one single person in that village in an endeavor to help them find the Savior! We just left them to God and God did it! That is why *you haven't a single backslider in that whole community.* Oh, my dear people, when God does a work, He does it well! You can go back, and you can go back again, and you'll find them pressing on with the God that revealed, not only Himself **to** them, but revealed Himself **in** them.

Salvation is of God

"God," said David, *"God is the God of our salvation."* The fact of ultimate reality surely is this, that salvation is of God!

I was asked recently to help a young woman. She was a nurse in Glasgow, now home in the Hebrides, and she was in terrible distress of soul, and the distress continued for a long period. Her father thought that perhaps a word from me might help her, so I called and I found the young woman in a terrible state, fearfully distressed about her soul. The sense of guilt, the sense of unworthiness, and behind it all, the question: "Am I in the covenant...Am I in the covenant?" So I knelt beside her and did my best to help her, and I quoted that great verse of Scripture that I so often quote, John 10:27, *"My sheep hear my voice and I know them and they follow me and I give unto them Eternal Life and they shall never perish, neither can any man pluck them out of my Father's hand."* And I quoted it again, and I tried to point out the two supreme characteristics of the sheep for whom Christ died. They hear his voice and they follow Him!

Have you heard His voice? Oh, have you heard His voice, young people? Have you heard His voice? It is different from the voice of man! The voice of the Shepherd speaking the word of conviction, speaking the word of pardon, speaking the word of assurance, speaking the word of power. Have you heard the voice of the Shepherd?

I spoke along these lines, and then she looked at me through her tears and said, "Mr. Campbell, I thank you for your kindly words of counsel, but surely, surely, as a minister, you believe that a verse of Scripture won't save you?"

Have you got it? Oh, have you got it?

Extensive Delusion About Salvation!

There are thousands today living under a self-created delusion, and a delusion given birth to in our evangelical crusades, who have nothing to rest upon but a verse of Scripture. Are you saved by a verse of Scripture?

Listen to the poet, "The promise can't save though the promise is sure. It is the blood we get under that cleanses us through. It cleanses me now. Hallelujah to God! I rest on the promise but I'm under the blood!" That's it! That's it! "Beyond...beyond...the sacred page I see Thee, Lord...I seek thee, Lord...my spirit yearns for Thee, thou living Word."

Tell me, has the living Word spoken? Has the living Word spoken, or are you just holding on to a verse of Scripture?

So she said, "Surely you are not suggesting that a verse of Scripture will save me? *"My heart cries for Jesus!"* That's it! *"My heart cries for Jesus!"* And Jesus, four or five days after that, revealed Himself **in** her...revealed Himself **in** her! And she was gloriously saved. And today she rests upon the promise, she feeds upon the Word—that brings her to Jesus.

Revival Where The Bible Is Unknown

Oh, let's get this clear. It is a truth we want to lay hold of. And it becomes so wonderfully real in revival. People have said to me, "But you see, Mr. Campbell, up there they know the Word of God and the Holy Spirit has ground to work on. They are not tied up with this doctrine and that doctrine and the other doctrine."

But listen friends. God sweeps into communities where the Word of God, to a large extent, is unknown. There are such communities in Britain, almost pagan. But I've seen God sweeping into such communities. For instance, the Midland of England just recently, sweeping into a godless community, and suddenly men and women understanding perfectly what it means to be born again and what it means to be sanctified, who, before the moving of God knew nothing or could not understand what Christ meant by saying, *"You must be born again."* That's why I say there's hope for any community when God takes the situation in hand.

MAN'S RESPONSIBILITY FOR REVIVAL

The origin then is God...and the way God works—I think we've seen that. But *His agents are His people.* God, as I have already said, is the God of revival. He is sovereign, but as I already said, I quote again, "we do not believe in any conception of sovereignty that nullifies my responsibility"...to say as many do today, "Well, we can do nothing, we've just to wait for the wind to blow." Well, that may be a very accommodating doctrine to the man at ease in Zion, but it will not stand in the light of Divine revelation.

"If my people, called by my name, will pray." I wonder how many of us are praying? I wonder how many of us here talking about revival and interested in the convention are giving time to God in prayer.

I'm thankful that I was brought up in a home where prayer had a prominent place. Mother saw that God had at least an hour every morning...stillness in the farm house. No work from half past six in the morning to half past seven. Horses fed at six. Oh, yes, they had to be attended to. (Those were the days of horses...and I'm not sure but what they were better days than the days in which we're living.) Half past six until half past seven...quietness in the farm house...in order that we might listen to God and give God an opportunity to speak to us.

We are the human agents through which revival is possible. Let me ask this question, *"Are you in the place where God can trust you with revival?"* He is sovereign. He is supernatural. But He comes down! And in His sovereign purpose and wise economy, He has placed this treasure in earthen vessels. Are you one that He can use? Are you one that He can trust? Are you in intimate fellowship with God?

I'm sure some of you will have heard of Murray McCheyne...died at twenty-seven, but left his mark, an indelible mark, on Scotland. Murray McCheyne was wonderfully used in revival prior to the disruption of '43. It was the revivals of McCheyne and Bonar and others that led to that great disruption when the free church left the establishment. Murray McCheyne said this, "If we are to walk worthy of our high and holy calling, we must live in daily consideration of the greatness and glory of Jesus."

The man who is there is just the man that God can trust with Revival. He is sovereign, but I am the instrument that He wills to use. Oh, tell me, friend, tell me, **are you there?**

PERSONAL TESTIMONY

Now, I want to close my talk by telling you something of how God in His mercy met with me. I must go back to the days of my conversion.

Conversion

I was converted under strange circumstances. I cannot take time to tell it all. But I was a piper and a step-dancer. And I was playing in a concert and dance outside of Oban when God spoke to me. God spoke to me in the dance. I had a praying father and a praying mother. And I left the dance and went home, shut myself in the barn and knelt among the straw prepared for the horses in the morning. And I cried, "God, I do not know how to come. I know not what to do, but if you'll save me as I am, I'm coming now." And God saved me! God saved me! And I say here today that never for one single moment had I ever any occasion to doubt the work that God did in my heart that morning. God did a sovereign and supernatural work and set me gloriously free. I believe that I can honestly say, Godliness... Godliness...characterized every part of my being— body, soul, and spirit—in that wonderful experience. And I'm not talking of sanctification or the deeper life. I'm just talking of a soul born again when God does the work.

A Defeated, Desperate Christian

But shortly after that I joined the forces and found myself in France during the 1st World War. And it wasn't long until I discovered that there were powers resident within me that were more than a match for me. You see, I was cradled in the midst of Godliness. And I found myself in the midst of extreme ungodliness—*extreme ungodliness.*

And I soon discovered, as I already said, forces resident within me that were more than a match for me. Again and again I cried, "Oh, God, speak the word of deliverance along with particular avenue."

Injured in Battle

However, to make a long story short, I am in a cavalry charge. And in that cavalry charge, I at last find myself lying on the battlefield, badly wounded.

I thank God for a young trooper of the Canadian Horses. (I owe a great deal to Canada. For that reason I am happy to be here to pay a long-standing debt.) I was lying on the ground when there was a second charge and this charge was by the Canadian Horses, the last Cavalry charge of the British Army...outside of Ales on the 12th of April, 1918. And, as they charged over that bloody field, a horse's hoof struck me in the spine. I must have groaned, and that groan registered in the mind of the young trooper that was in the charge, so much so, that in the providence of God, he came right back to where I lay. After they had cleared the hill and took the guns, he came back, dismounted, and threw me across the horse's back and carried me to the first casualty clearing station. I thank God for that young man, whomever or wherever he is.

Desperate for Holiness: Endued with Power

I, on that horse's back, entered into an experience that revolutionized my life. I believed that I was dying. I knew that I was being carried to the casualty clearing station, but would I ever see it? And I prayed a prayer frequently prayed by my father, "God, make me as holy as a saved sinner can be." That was it! McCheyne's prayer—"Make me as holy as a saved sinner can be." And listen, friends, God swept into my life! God, the Holy Ghost—I cannot explain it in any other way—swept into my life as I was brought to the station.

Now, listen, I could not speak very much English then. Gaelic was my language. But I know this, that I began to talk about Jesus in Gaelic...in Gaelic...and there wasn't a soul there that could understand me. And I want to say this, that before we left that casualty clearing station, seven Canadians were gloriously saved—seven of them!

Midargyl Revival

Again, I must leave that casualty clearing station and after a year in the hospital, and after a few months of Bible training, I went out to proclaim the unsearchable riches of Jesus. It was the Midargyl Revival. God moved in those parishes in a mighty way and hundreds were swept into the Kingdom of God.

Defeated Again

And then an evil hour struck me. I *stepped consciously out of the will of God!* I began to study for the ministry. And I'm sorry to say that during that period I drifted far from God in my mind...in my mind and in my heart. Oh, I was still evangelical, passed through, came out a minister, and for seventeen years ministered to two congregations.

I was Campbell of the Midargyl Revival and I would be asked to address conventions and conferences. Oh, the deceit of the human heart! I knew how unfit I was. Oh, I would question my salvation, because I tried to live consistently. But I knew barrenness...barrenness...in *my spirit.*

Prayer became a burden and the Word of God a dead word. Oh, brother, have you had that experience?

Desperate Again

Then one day...oh, how I thank God for that day...my young daughter came to me...thank God for her...a girlie of sixteen years of age—she came to me and said, "Daddy, I would like to see you in your study. I've been praying for you, Daddy. I want to speak to you." And she took me to my study, and she threw herself on my knees, as daughters sometimes do. She put her arms around my neck, and I can still see the tears streaming from her eyes, as she said, "Daddy, when you were a pilgrim in the Faith Mission, after the 1st World War, you saw revival in Scotland. You saw revival! Daddy, how is it that God is not using you in revival today? Tell me, Daddy, when did you last lead a soul to Christ?"

Thank God for faithful daughters! And I tell you, dear people, that shook me. Oh, it shook me! I knew! I knew! Campbell, a convention speaker...Campbell, the evangelistic minister...in his study smashed and broken by a question from his daughter.

Listen, I was booked to address the Keswick Convention that year. I went to the convention. Oh, the deceit of the human heart. I went to the convention and I had my address. And I was so thankful when it was over. The words kept ringing in my ears,

"When did you last lead a soul to Christ? When did you last lead a soul to Christ?"

Determined to Leave the Ministry

Then God in His own wonderful way moved Dr. Tom Fitch to depart from the address that he had prepared and give his own personal testimony. Dr. Fitch gave his personal testimony and I went home resolved that unless God would do something for me and give me back what I lost, that *I certainly would resign from the ministry.* I was absolutely decided on that!

So, in going home, I said to my wife and daughter, "I'm going to my study and I want you to leave me alone. I'm going to seek a meeting with God."

And I went to my study. I shut the door. I put the rug down on the floor in front of the fire and I lay on the rug. I cannot take time to tell you all that God said to me in that hour. I'm thankful to say that He spoke to me the word of pardon, and the word of forgiveness, and the word of re-commission.

I cried, "God, won't you give me again what you gave me on the battlefield?" And listen, friends, God did it!

My daughter came in at 2:00 in the morning. She lay down beside me and she said, "Daddy, whatever it costs, go through with God." And I said, "Sheena, I'm going through whatever it may cost."

Cost to Pride

And God knows what it cost me—to stand in my

pulpit the following Sunday and make a public apology for pretending what I was not in the midst of my congregation. Five of my office bearers left me within a week. They wouldn't have a fool in the pulpit.

Oh, that may happen. It sometimes happens, you see, in revival, that there's a subtraction before addition.

Baptized with Love and Power

But listen, friends, as I lay there, God the Holy Ghost came upon me. *Wave after wave came rolling over me until the love of God swept through me like a mighty river!* So much so, that there were moments...now listen, my daughter beside me put her hand on my shoulders and she prayed, "Oh, God, keep his reason to Daddy." I was never more sane in my life! But I was so wrought upon by the Holy Ghost that I cried and I laughed and I prayed.

No Gift of Tongues

Someone asked me, "Did you speak in tongues?" Oh, I was asked that again and again. No, my dear people, I've never spoken in tongues nor have I ever been in a meeting where tongues have been practiced.

But I say that the Holy Ghost came to me...in a mighty cleansing, empowering power!

A professor in Edinburgh met me sometime afterward. Of course, it was known abroad that something had happened to Campbell. (Of course, something did happen to him. I was set free—glorious freedom!) This professor said to me, "Now tell me, tell me, Campbell...they tell me that you had a wonderful experience in your study."

"Yes," I said. "God came to me."

"What difference did it make in your life?"

"Well, I think, professor, that the difference must be obvious to you from what has already happened," I said. "I went out to preach the same sermons that I'd been preaching for seventeen years...went out to preach the same sermons with this difference—that I now saw hundreds converted, hundreds brought savingly to Christ."

Go Through With God

And if God in His mercy has been pleased to use me in some small measure since that hour, I can trace it back to that moment, when Sheena said to me, "Whatever it costs, Daddy, go through with God."

And I say to you, brother, whatever it costs...whatever it costs...go through with God!

WHAT SHALL WE DO?

A spirit of repentance marked the life of Duncan Campbell. How easily God broke him through a mere sentence from the lips of his teenage daughter!

If the message of Duncan Campbell has found a lodging place in your heart and will not leave you alone, perhaps the Lord is about the process of helping you "break up your fallow ground" that He might work revival in your life. It is fairly easy to remove the outer layers of sin in our hearts. Total cleansing requires painful honesty before God, however. True repentance involves dealing with sin itself and its horrible offense toward a Holy God. It is not simply a matter of facing sin's consequences. There is Godly sorrow that leads to repentance; there is the sorrow of the world that results only in death. The convicting work of the Spirit of God is always sin-specific; that is, the Lord does not produce a general feeling of wrong, but a very specific labeling of our words, attitudes, actions, or motives as sin in light of the dazzling white righteousness of Jesus Christ.

As the Lord moves upon your heart, like Duncan Campbell, you must "seek a meeting with God." Examine your heart before Him. Determine the motives of your heart, as revealed by that which tempts you. Identify the worldly pleasures that distract you from Christ. Seek to know how you have grieved God's Spirit. Become conscious that God observes and weighs every thought, word, attitude, and deed of your life. Define the specific teachings of God's Word which you are violating. Bare your heart before the Lord; then seek His forgiveness, and that of others. Make necessary restitutions. Be willing to humble yourself and to go to any lengths to set things right before God and your brother.

God **will** meet with you, as He met with Duncan Campbell. He will take your failures and wash them in Christ's precious Blood, then use them to build a fresh message of His grace through your life to others. Will you dare to join Campbell and **"go through with God"?**

Cassettes
REVIVAL RESOURCES!!
Soul-stirring accounts of God-breathed awakenings

Tape #1 **The Lewis Revival** by Duncan Campbell
Thrilling account of a 3-year revival where thousands were converted and conviction swept through the Hebrides. God stepped down from Heaven!

Tape #2 **The Turkey Creek Revival** by J. D. Brogdon
Astonishing story of God visiting a small North Carolina community in 1963. 2000 gathered nightly in a church which only seated 300.

Tape #3 **The Canadian Revival** by Bill McLeod
In 1971 a revival broke out in western Canada. The crowds swelled from 190 to 4000 during seven weeks! Pastor McLeod shares how the Lord prepared him to prepare the church for this great outpouring. (Great insights for pastors)

Tape #4 **The Shantung Revival** by C. L. Culpeper
This veteran missionary shares how revival came to China as the missionaries humbled themselves and sought the Lord.

Tape #5 **Lewis—Land of Revival** (Ambassador Productions)
Here are testimonies from those who were touched by God in this extraordinary movement on the island of Lewis.

Cassette Tapes: $5.00 each
All Five in Album $28.00 postpaid

Quantity Prices for
The Nature of a God-Sent Revival

Single copy: $2.50 plus $1.00 handling
Ten to Twenty-Five copies: $1.75 each plus $3.00 handling
Twenty-Five or more copies: $1.50 each plus $4.00 handling
Fifty or more copies $1.25 each plus $5.00 handling

Quantity		Total
_____	The Nature of a God-Sent Revival...............	$_____
_____	Revival Tape Album $28.00........................	$_____
_____	The Price and Power of Revival by Duncan Campbell $3.50.............................	$_____

VA Residents add 4 1/2 % sales tax........................... $_____

Postage (Minimum $1.50)....................................... $_____

TOTAL.....$_____

Make checks payable to: **Christ Life Publications**
P.O. Box 399, Vinton, VA 24179

Name _____

Address_____

City, State, Zip _____